Architectural Signatures Canada

atelier BUILD

TUNS PRESS

Tuns Press
Faculty of Architecture and Planning
Dalhousie University
Halifax, Nova Scotia, Canada
Web: tunspress.dal.ca

Editorial Board
Grant Wanzel
Essy Baniassad
Brian Carter
Steven Mannell
Stephen Parcell
Donald Westin

Atelier BUILD
Editor: Brian Carter
Production: Donald Westin
Printing: Friesens

© 2010 by Tuns Press
All Rights Reserved. Published January 2010
Printed in Canada

Canadian Cataloguing in Publication

Carroll, Michael, 1964-
Atelier BUILD / Michael Carroll,
Danita Rooyakkers; [editor, Brian Carter].

ISBN 978-0-929112-57-2

1. Atelier BUILD. 2. Architecture –
Québec (Province) – Montréal – 21st
century. I. Rooyakkers, Danita
II. Carter, Brian, 1942- III. Title.

NA749.B84C37 2010
720.92'271428   C2008-905941-7

atelier BUILD

- 16 Thin House
- 22 Tower House
- 26 Back House
- 30 Box House
- 38 EcoCité Habitat I
- 46 Super 8
- 52 @Mentana
- 56 Fernhill Urban Cottages

7	Foreword
8	*Urban Interventions*
10	*Poetic/Pragmatic Symbiosis*
12	*The Workings*
36	Code : Zero
59	Postscript
60	Acknowledgements
62	Credits
63	Contributors

Foreword
Grant Wanzel

Every new publication is a source of pleasure for us. However, as this is also the first book in a new series, the present volume carries double the pleasure.

Architectural Signatures Canada is a series that is complementary to our continuing series *Documents in Canadian Architecture*. While a book in this series may differ from our other publications, our philosophy remains unchanged. Both will continue to offer insights into the process of design by documenting the facts and products of the process: the sketches, drawings, models, mock-ups – and the results. Text will be free of rhetoric and self-promotion. The architecture will stand on its own, open to critical reflection and serious study.

This new series and this particular book continue our determination to present the unvarnished facts of the work, established in early Tuns Press publications. We do so out of the firm conviction that it is the 'good bones' of fine architecture that are of most interest to students of the discipline. In this respect, while the work of Atelier Build is modest in scale and highly focused in scope, it bears close scrutiny. Each and every project in this portfolio is important for its ambition, no less so for its achievement.

This is searching work, clever in the ways that it seeks out and reveals the potential of overlooked sites and under-utilized situations. 'Spec-building', ever a tough business, is usually associated with 'quick and dirty' outcomes. Atelier Build offers a compelling alternative, and in the process makes the difficult seem easy.

The work of Atelier Build has much to teach us about city-building, housing, real estate, finance, accomplished design, and their interdependence. With this publication, Atelier Build invites us into a world of high risk and dizzying complexity.

Urban Interventions
Brian Carter

Thin House, 1996, Atelier Build

The group of religious mystics who came to Canada from France almost fifty years after the founding of Cap Diamant by Champlain in 1608, and their commitment to build a missionary city in the wilderness, defined a site as the place that was eventually to become the City of Montreal. That historic settlement was to grow under the direction of a series of different administrations and religious influences to become one of Canada's most significant cities and an important centre of commerce, government and education in North America.

Today it is a place still conspicuously shaped by the natural landscape yet at the same time by a physical form that also clearly reflects those unique and different cultural histories. Dense blocks of building define distinct districts and constitute a substantial inventory of space – space that accommodates housing and trade, civic activities and public uses. It is a mix that is vital to the formation of lively urban neighbourhoods defined by extensive and elegant networks of streets and squares. Connected by an infrastructure of civic spaces and public institutions, civic amenities, landscape and public transportation systems these together recall the city's European roots and combine to radically transform that original wilderness.

This is a distinctly urban fabric that is intricate, well-used and valued and which, in turn, continues to shape the design of the many notable new buildings that have been built there. And whilst it is complemented by the monumental modernism of Ernest Cormier, the more recent reconstruction of the City of Montreal is characterized by the work of other architects – Dan Hanganu, Peter Rose, Saucier and Perrotte, Jacques Rousseau and many more who, together with their clients, have frequently focused on the renovation and re-use of existing buildings as an integral part of the creation of new urban artifacts.

And while the design of projects, like the Canadian Centre for Architecture, the Cinémathèque Québécoise on the Boulevard de Maisonneuve and the Pointe-à-Callière Archeological Museum alongside Place Royal, have each involved the recognition of notable landmarks, adaption of existing buildings and the sensitive design of new alongside historic urban fragments, they have consequently ensured a sustained respect for, and continued confrontation with, history in this city. It is an approach that some architects of a younger generation have also enthusiastically recognised as they have gone on to make this particularly unique place the territory for their own subsequent investigations.

Atelier Build has been working creatively within these constraints for the last decade. Prompted by modest interventions in Montreal, and inspired by their own individual experiences and new buildings they have discovered in other similarly dense and conspicuously well-used cities including Tokyo and Amsterdam, this practice, directed by two young designers, has developed an impressive portfolio of small buildings.

Danita Rooyakkers and Michael Carroll both studied in Nova Scotia in the mid-1980s and Brian MacKay-Lyons was one of their professors. A notable designer, MacKay-Lyons is sometimes characterized as a 'village architect'. In fact it is often the urban building that MacKay-Lyons pioneered in Halifax and not the more frequently published and photogenic 'huts' constructed on remote headlands overlooking the ocean, which seems to have shaped the work and attitudes of others among the designers that have followed.

At a moment in time when the icon frequently dominates discussions about architecture and cities, this particular approach focuses on a city of very different bits. It presents an alternative approach that recalls the work and writings of Aldo Rossi, the significance of 'urban artifacts' and of learning from existing landscapes. Preoccupied with the rapid growth of the city and the resultant urban form, Rossi underlined the value and relevance of historic building types in his influential book *The Architecture of the City*. MacKay-Lyons' work in Halifax presents a range of projects that infilled spaces between, took lessons from buildings that had existed in the locality and ingeniously combined the populist ideas of Charles Moore, MacKay-Lyons' own teacher at UCLA, with the writings of Robert Venturi and Aldo Rossi that shaped architectural discourse in the late sixties. The planning and design of projects utilized familiar house forms – the row house, corner block, and carriage house, and many of these ideas can be seen to have shaped the subsequent approach of Atelier Build.

Atelier Build has developed those ideas through a series of projects that they have designed and built in Montreal. Their work has been focused in that city and utilized often unlikely sites in a creative effort to re-instate historic urban fabrics. In making a commitment to build in a particular city, they have also chosen to work in a way that integrates design with development, building with prevailing market forces and combining the new with the old.

This is a remarkably complex role for designers to take on, yet it is one that has enabled this emerging practice to define new territory and help rebuild the historic city while also demonstrating the value and potential of the urban artifact and its importance as an alternative to the icon.

Poetic / Pragmatic Symbiosis
Michael Carroll

The architect of the future – if he wants to rise to the top again – will be forced by the trend of events to draw closer once more to the building production. If he will build up a closely co-operating team together with the engineer, the scientist, and the builder, then design construction and economy may again become an entity – a fusion of art, science and business.[1]
Walter Gropius

Atelier Build began in 1995, prompted by a desire to make architecture that bridged the divide between the studio and the construction site. This would be accomplished by creating a series of design-build projects which argued for a leaner, more urbane architecture for contemporary city life.

Although piecemeal and domestic in scale, the individual projects are directed towards a more ambitious goal – the collective act of making a city. Through a series of interstitial interventions on marginal sites, the projects attempt to repair and strengthen the coherence of the urban block, add to its formal and material complexity, and increase the density and diversity of its inhabitants.

Given the urban agenda, the projects, although residential in scope, challenge accepted notions of domesticity. The spatial configurations in plan and section provide a flexibility that accommodates a range of live/work scenarios: the professional who wants a street-front studio; the modern-day family whose members demand varying degrees of independence. From the 'vertical loft' of the Thin House with its interior unit widths of eleven feet, to the stacked townhouses on rue Mentana with their street-front, double-height volumes and sleeping lofts, the projects push the boundaries of conventional housing and offer alternatives to an urban population.

In 2004/2005 Atelier Build was awarded the Canadian Prix de Rome, enabling us to travel and to study two mature, material cultures: Japan and the Netherlands. This experience enabled us to re-situate our work within an international context, and to refresh our architectural imaginations with a range of projects and landscapes that inspire our enterprise in the North American inner city.

Traditional architecture in Japan – as seen in the temples, shrines, tea houses, and in the pleasure palaces created for the wealthy – makes great and subtle use of spatial depth and emphasis on the space 'in-between'. Arata Isozaki in his book *Japan-ness in Architecture* speaks about the Japanese concepts of time and space rooted etymologically with the Chinese ideogram *ma* – the interstice. [2] The Imperial Villa Katsura (circa 1620) is an often-cited and stellar example of these ideas, as it consists of a series of layered spaces comprised of movable screens and verandahs situated amidst the sublime beauty of its gardens. The landscaping surrounding such structures is considered an integral part of the structure itself.

In Japan, our research focused on the work of Atelier Bow-Wow, comprised of Momoyo Kaijima and Yoshiharu Tsukamoto, who have been at the forefront of investigating the interstices of the generic Tokyo urban block. They acknowledge the strong poetic sensibility of the culture and incorporate traditional aspects of Japanese architecture while working within the constraints of the contemporary city. Their books, *Pet Architecture Guide Book* and *Made In Tokyo*, provided an initial guide for Atelier Build to seek out the architectural anomalies of Tokyo's quirky urban vernacular. Their projects, some sited in the margins of Tokyo, seem to teeter between background fabric and architectural object. In the case of Kadoya 315, for example, a five-storey mixed-use project in suburban Tokyo, the form of the building 'steps forward' towards the street to announce its foreground status.

In contrast to the poetics of Japanese architecture, an arguably more pragmatic sensibility is evident in contemporary Dutch architecture, with its array of innovative housing, particularly in the post-industrial docklands of Amsterdam and other areas such as Almere and Breda.

Given the playful yet pragmatic sensibility inherent in the work of Atelier Build, and given Danita Rooyakker's Dutch

heritage, the Netherlands provided insight for both past and future projects. We explored a wide range, from John Hejduk's idiosyncratic Wall House 2 in Groningen to OMA's courtyard housing on a former military base in Breda. Other works, such as the Schröder House by Gerrit Rietveld in Utrecht, were inspirational in their design of flexible space – here achieved by a series of sliding and folding doors that subdivide the second floor living space into private sleeping areas at night. Just to the east of the house is a lesser-known project designed by Rietveld: the Erasmuslaan 9 Housing Block, built in the early 1930s, whose stripped-down apartments resonate with Atelier Build's Super 8 project.

In Amsterdam, a series of projects along the waterfront offer a remarkable variety of urban housing that has revitalized an entire edge of the city. Whether it is MVRDV's ten-storey Silodam project, situated on the end of a pier in the western docklands, or the developments located on Java-eiland, KNSM-eiland, and the Borneo and Sporenburg Peninsulas, the developments in Amsterdam demonstrate how housing, designed in an elegant and consistent manner, can transform a city. Such housing is a model not only for Europe but also for North America.

Contemporary Dutch architecture has fostered a strong design culture that is eminently exportable. Many of these projects, in their emphasis on frugal yet comfortable domestic space and their focus on re-using what is already available, resonate with the formal and social aspirations of Atelier Build. At the same time, at Atelier Build we have a 'Japanese' passion for the synergy of outer and inner spaces. In our use of materials that echo the surrounding environment, of roof-gardens and balconies, portals and windows that frame' local landmarks or places of beauty, we create truly alternative urban dwellings.

Our body of work, inspired by our Prix de Rome travels, articulates an architectural position centered on innovative urban housing strategies that embrace the contemporary city. As a design-build studio we like to think of our work inspiring other design practitioners to maximize architecture's true potential, negotiating the thinking and making divide with a sensibility that embraces both the pragmatic and poetic – that infuses the everyday with a sense that something extraordinary is but a moment away.

[1] *Architectural Forum* 96 (May 1952): 111.
[2] Arata Isozaki, *Japan-ness in Architecture*, (Cambridge, Mass.: MIT Press, 2006).

Photos – top to bottom:
Teahouse, Imperial Villa of Katsura
Kadoya 315, Atelier Bow-Wow, Tokyo
Erasmuslaan Apartment, Gerrit Rietveld, Utrecht
Borneo-Sporenburg, West 8, Amsterdam

The Workings
Danita Rooyakkers

@Mentana, 2008, Atelier Build

The mid-nineteen-nineties was a time of growing political tension and economic turmoil in Quebec. As a result, the opportunities for young architects to gain experience by working in established practices there were limited. Also, at this time, residential development in Montreal was primarily developer-driven, and the architect was often seen as the provider of the drawings required to secure building permits. Consequently, the professional development offered in this setting, along with the importance attributed to design, was minimal.

At this time the potential of available development sites often was also compromised by the need to offer properties for quick sale, and consequently building designs tended to be formulaic and focused on a handful of standardized prototypes. These conditions often combined in ways that limited options of prospective clients.

Provoked by these issues, Michael Carroll and I concluded that an alternative approach to the conventional practice of architecture was necessary, and possible. With an initiative fostered by this vision, and by our desire and need to act independently on a different platform, we formed the design-build partnership of Atelier Build.

Opting to work primarily in the Plateau district of Montreal, we undertook to organize the complete development of several projects. By designing and contracting to build a project ourselves, we were able to have complete control. Our business model evolved and the attention to detail that we were able to bring to that work began to define an alternative approach to design, construction and the development of new buildings. We were not driven solely by maximizing profit and sought to develop a model that integrated the value of design and architecture of quality with efficient construction and development at a fundamental level. Having control over both design and construction provided flexibility. It also offered new opportunities to make changes during the construction phase. This, in turn, made it possible in certain circumstances to customize projects for clients. This way of working created an operating dynamic within Atelier Build in which the traditional boundaries of architectural practice were broadened.

Our first projects defied the conventional rationale of speculative development in an economic downturn. As we persevered, gained experience and garnered support, the housing industry in Montreal also began to take on a new momentum. After the Referendum, the city experienced a major recovery with a housing boom supported by new funding for different kinds of projects. In this context we promoted the idea that good design, all too often reserved for large scale projects and privately commissioned houses, could also be directed at small-scale residential buildings. This also encouraged local people not only to reconsider good design but make it an important part of their everyday lives. Consequently Montreal, with its diverse and vibrant cultural settings, began to provide a place for innovative architectural practice while the dense urban fabric of the city offered new opportunities to develop infill projects and design new small residential buildings on unconventional, and previously overlooked, urban sites.

As urban development became increasingly valued, both economically and ecologically, so new potential development sites became obvious. Buildings that had been burned out or boarded up were re-examined, while tiny leftover sites and solitary buildings on large lots attracted renewed attention. Atelier Build carried out assessments of market value, municipal zoning and building regulations at the same time that we acquired sites, examined their development potential and prepared design options. It was an integrative approach that brought together design, development and construction.

It created workdays that included scouting for potential sites on foot as well as by bicycle and through the internet, initiated intensive periods of design study and planning so as to evaluate the potential of particular sites, prompted collaborations with other professionals, suppliers and technical consultants as well as visits to sites to resolve problems related to buildings already under construction, to notaries and to financiers.

The result of this way of working has been the creation of new residential and mixed-use buildings that are affordable, and well designed and that also re-use land and existing buildings. It is a satisfactory way of working that re-affirms our position in the life of a particular city and culture through the advocacy of good design, effective planning and thoughtful construction.

Projects

Thin House
MONTREAL, 1996

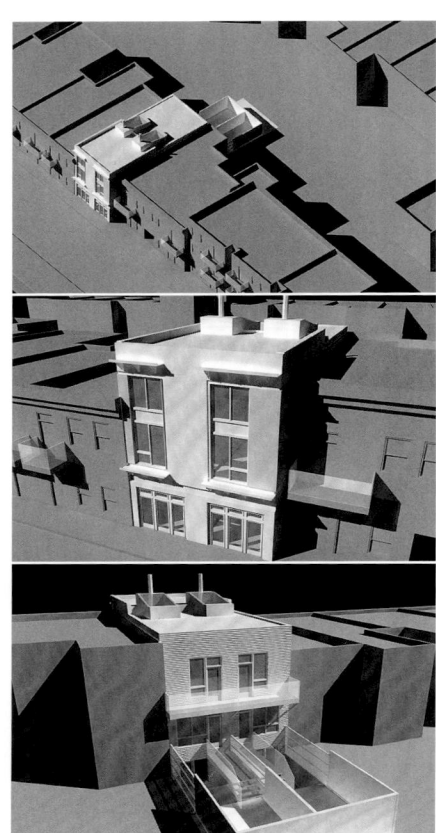

THIN HOUSE : *3,000 SF. DUPLEX, AVENUE DE L'HÔTEL-DE-VILLE*

Thin House is an experiment that challenges the Montreal norm of horizontally divided flats. Occupying a narrow site in the densely built neighbourhood of Plateau Mont-Royal, each of the two units, mirrored along a dividing wall, is a narrow, vertical house that is fifty-six feet long and less than eleven feet wide.

The vertical division offered a successful approach for developing other narrow, marginal sites. As a basic scheme, the plan allowed an entry door at street level, an enclosed back garden and generous skylights for both units. Initially, the floor plates were to be continuous, but with the site's high water table and clay soil, the floor levels were split, allowing the back of the duplex to dig into the ground, and the front to incorporate a street-level garage, in accordance with the City's requirement for on-site parking. The split permitted six floor levels and a central thirty-five-foot-high atrium that allows natural light to infiltrate the middle zone of the house.

Thin House's design tempers a zero-detailing philosophy with a heterogeneous mix of materials. Exposed wooden joists in one area contrast with slightly canted drywall ceilings in another. MDF cabinetry gives way to dark blue laminate and hardwood veneer plywood. For the front elevation, commercial grade aluminum windows are matched with architectural grade concrete block, subdivided with galvanized C-channels that provide brackets for brick insets. Folded metal cornices bolted to the masonry façade provide a hint of the house's back elevation, which is clad in corrugated metal siding, with balconies and two metal stairs constructed of expanded metal mesh.

In the end, the strength of the house resides in its spatial complexity. The design emphasizes section over plan and volume over area, while the qualitative aspects of the design override the dimensional restrictions of the site. The result is a thin vertical loft, with a complex array of varying ceiling heights that seems more spacious than its narrow width suggests.

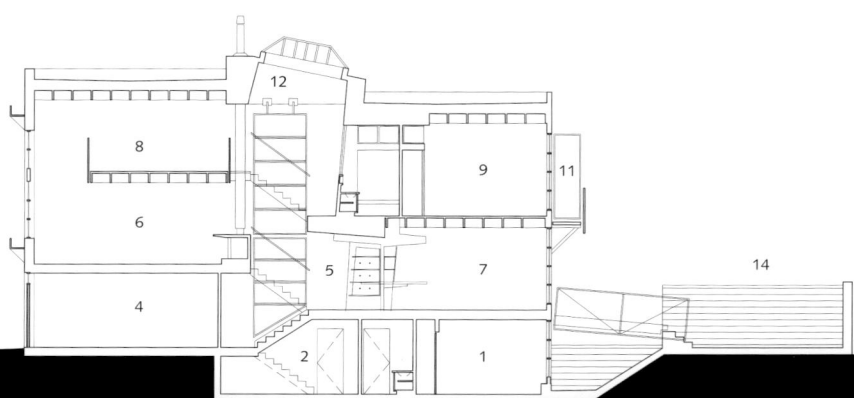

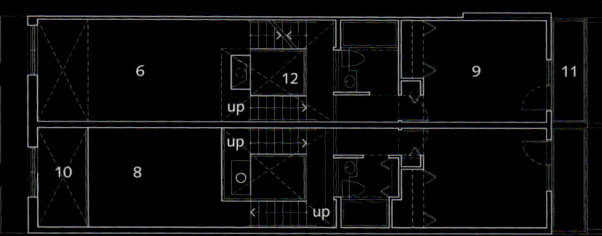

Third + fourth floor + mezzanine levels

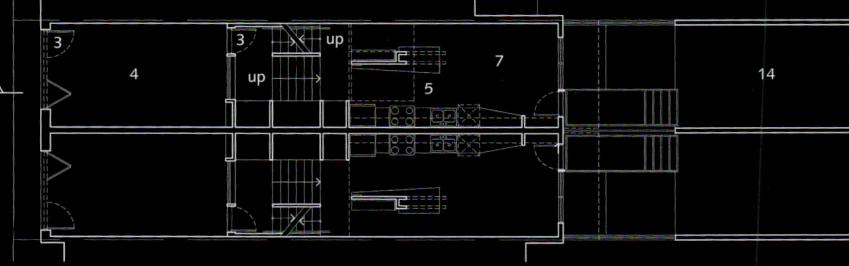

Garage + second floor levels

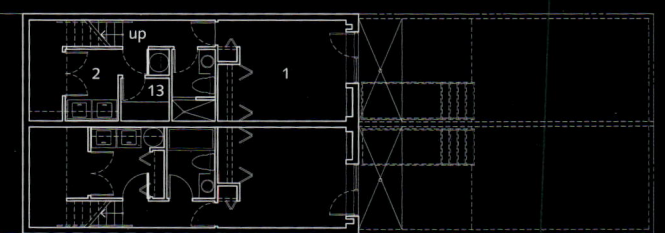

Basement level

1 Guest room / office
2 Laundry
3 Entry
4 Garage / studio
5 Kitchen
6 Living
7 Dining
8 Mezzanine
9 Bedroom
10 Open
11 Balcony
12 Stairwell / lightwell
13 Dry sauna
14 Garden

0   10'   20'

Tower House
MONTREAL, 1997

ATELIER BUILD 23

TOWER HOUSE : *4,500 SF. THREE UNIT CONDOMINIUM, AVENUE LAVAL*

Tower House is situated on one of Montreal's most intimate and historic streets. Although it was necessary to align the building with the existing datum of the street's ornate cornices and an adjacent building's piano nobile base, the project challenges its historical context with an industrial palette of materials that includes concrete block, corrugated metal siding, an expanded metal mesh balcony, folded galvanized metal cornices, and oversized windows with anodized aluminum frames.

Beyond this context, access to natural light was a challenge, given the compact nature of the corner lot, ninety-percent lot coverage, and a northwest exposure. The design solution was to create two towers, separated by a narrow, rhomboid-shaped court that is lined with reflective corrugated siding. This allows for large, vertically proportioned corner windows for each four-storey tower. To further augment natural daylight, two rooftop projections with industrial skylights are placed above a light well that is fitted with an open-riser stair and expanded metal mesh landings.

Although initially designed as a four-unit condominium, the south tower was sold during construction and consolidated into one unit, allowing space for a one-car garage accessed through the side laneway. The other tower remains divided. A small one-bedroom unit, with a tiny garden, forms the north tower's ground floor. The upper unit features a double-height living room with a mezzanine, and a stair leading to a rooftop terrace that has a full view of Mont-Royal Park and, at night, a roofscape of illuminated skylights.

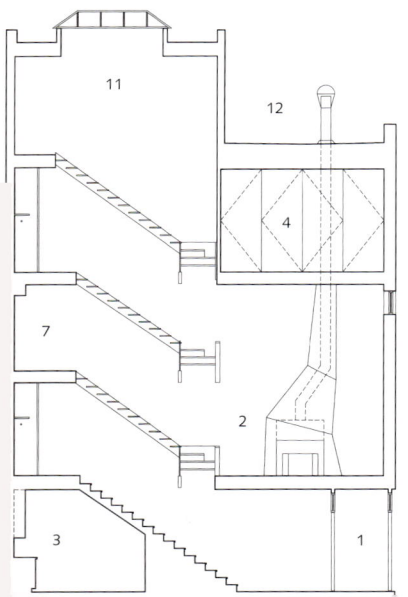

1 Entry
2 Living / dining
3 Kitchen
4 Bedroom
5 Guest room / office
6 Garage
7 Mezzanine
8 Open
9 Steel mesh walkway
10 Balcony
11 Stairwell / lightwell
12 Rooftop terrace

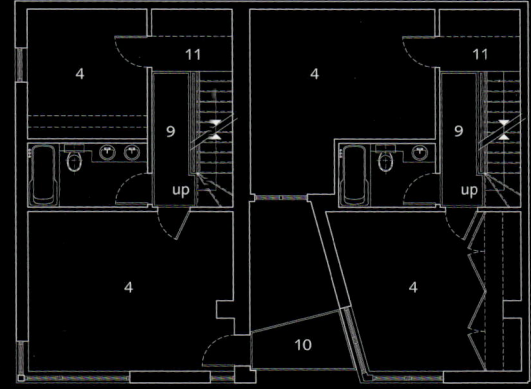

Fourth floor

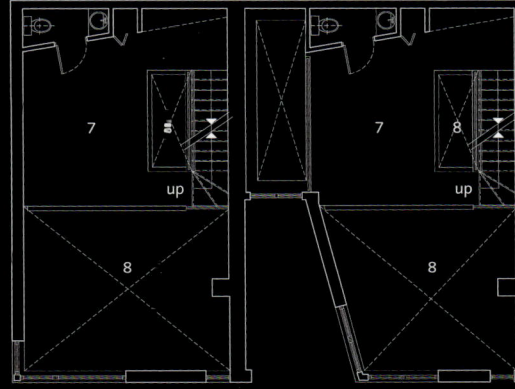

Third floor – mezzanine

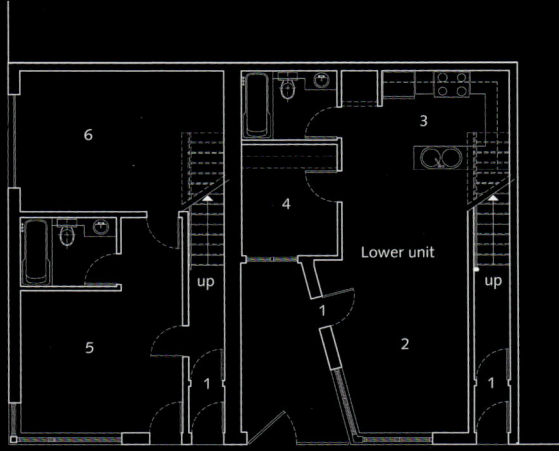

First floor – entry level

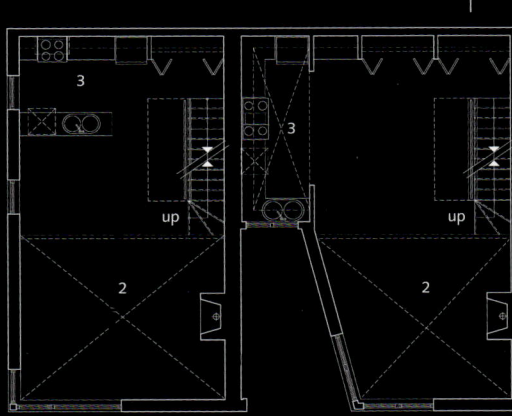

Second floor

Back House
MONTREAL, 1998

BACK HOUSE : *3,000 SF. DUPLEX, RUE ST-CHRISTOPHE*

Back House fronts onto a narrow, one-lane street that was formerly a service lane for rue Saint-Hubert, which lies directly to the southwest. A recent change in the City by-laws, which now allows construction of dwellings to replace existing garages, made the project possible. The project encompassed the renovation of a large house on rue Saint-Hubert and the construction of a new duplex at the back of the lot, replacing the existing garage on rue St-Christophe. The units are each eleven feet wide and thirty-five feet long, with four storeys comprising three floors and a mezzanine. A narrow central passage, lined with corrugated metal siding, leads from the street to an inner court that separates the new construction from the existing house.

The ground floor of each unit is comprised of a live/work studio, a half-bath, and a rear terrace connected to the street by a central passage. The second floor of each side is compact, with a small dining room at the back, an elongated galley kitchen in the middle, and a double-height living area at the front. This room, like the third floor bedroom above, has French doors with a shallow balcony that opens onto the street and offers oblique views to the neighbourhood square of Place Roy. Viewed from this square, Back House has a certain background status.

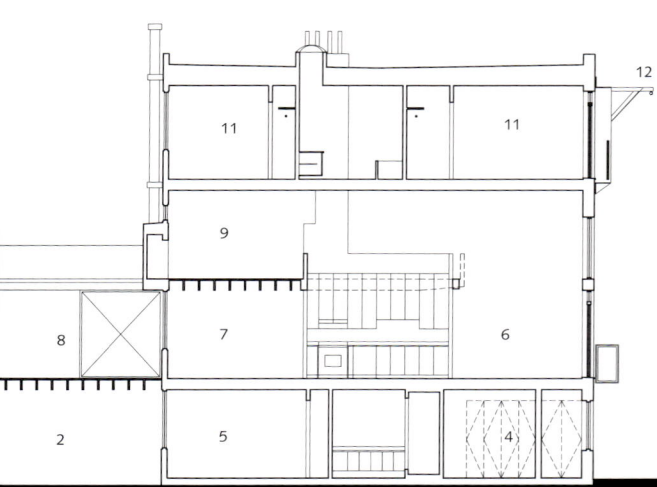

1. Existing house
2. Terrace
3. Breezeway
4. Entry
5. Office / bedroom
6. Living
7. Dining
8. Balcony
9. Family
10. Open
11. Bedroom
12. Furniture hoist

Fourth floor

Third floor – mezzanine

Second floor

First floor – entry level

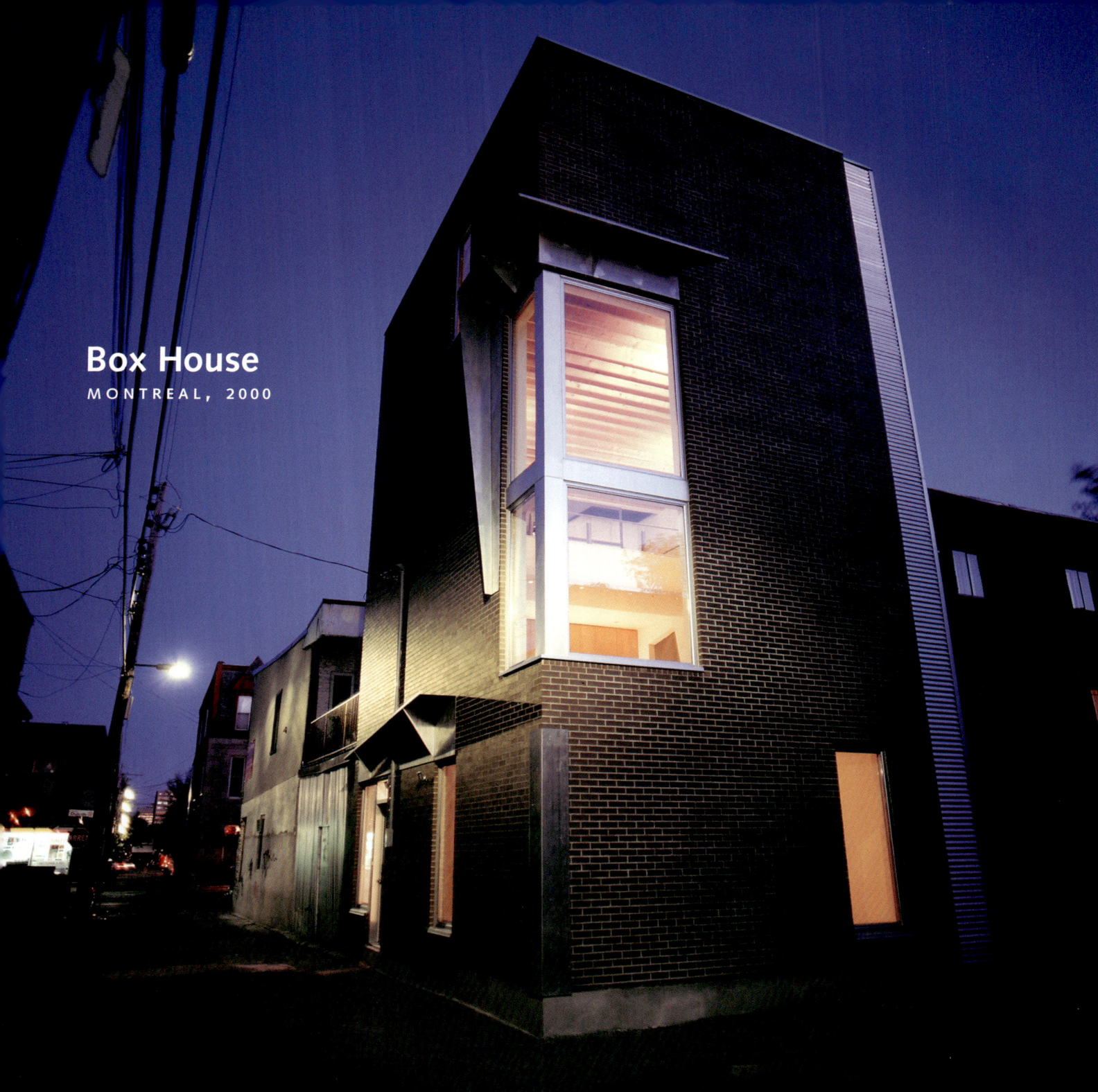

Box House
MONTREAL, 2000

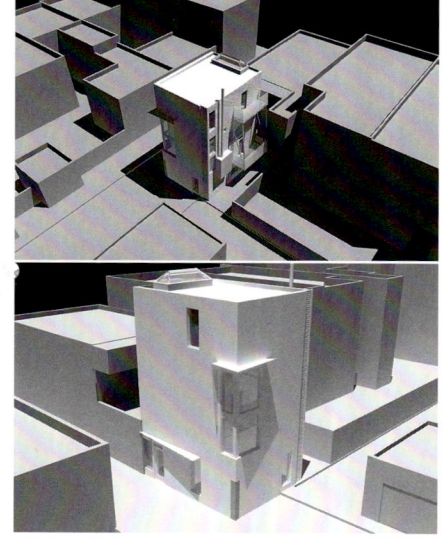

BOX HOUSE : *1,500 SF. SEMI-DETACHED HOUSE*

The Box House is situated at the corner of an alleyway and a narrow lane in the heart of Montreal's Plateau Mont-Royal. The site marks the point where the width of the lane is reduced by half. The house is literally in the middle of the street. The Box House occupies the margin.

The envelope is a rectangular box with metal appendages. The openings in the box are carefully scribed. The ground floor's north window marks the end of a sidewalk. The double-height corner window with a folded metal visor makes an urban gesture to the street and offers a view northward down the middle of the laneway. The triple-height slot window on the house's west side captures the afternoon sun and provides a view of the illuminated cross that sits on top of the mountain at Mont-Royal Park, from the third floor.

The house oscillates between an industrial and a domestic sensibility. The double-height living space with its mezzanine is zoned between a ground floor studio and a third-storey bedroom with ensuite bath. A thirty-six-foot-high stairwell, lit by an industrial skylight overhead, connects these spaces. Throughout the house, metal frame screens, expanded metal mesh landings and sheet metal stairs add to the industrial aesthetic.

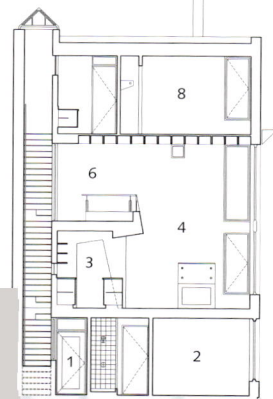

This is the record of a box man.
I am beginning this account in a box. A cardboard box that reaches just to my hips when I put it on over my head.
...
The greatest care must be taken when making the observation window. First decide on its size and location .... Ideally, the upper edge of the window will be six inches from the top of the box, and the lower edge eleven inches below that; the width will be seventeen inches. ...[T]he upper edge of the window comes to the eyebrows.
...
Just making the box is simple enough; at the outside it takes less than an hour. However, it requires considerable courage to put the box on, over your head, and get to be a box man.

Kobo Abe, *The Box Man* (New York: Alfred Knopf, 1974), 3, 5, 7.

1 Entry
2 Office / bedroom
3 Kitchen
4 Living / dining
5 Balcony
6 Mezzanine
7 Open
8 Bedroom
9 Patio

CODE : ZERO, 2002

This is an architectural installation designed for the Canadian Centre for Architecture's exhibition *Laboratoires* that opened in April, 2002. Atelier Build was one of six design ateliers that participated in the show, which was curated by Mark Wigley and Frédéric Migayrou. The installation was meant as a commentary on the state of architecture in a post-9-11 world.

Situated in Room 5 of the CCA, the installation was designed as an 'extended threshold' that was meant to engage and destabilize the participant. Eighty aluminium rods with two-inch-square cross-sections, and fourteen feet in length, were hung from the ceiling to create a double 'curtain wall' and form a narrow corridor. As each person passed through the space, the rods would move slightly and produce a noise as the hollow rods clanged against each other.

The second component of the installation was a 'dropped ceiling' comprised of an industrial 'silk' screen that measured five and a half feet by seventeen feet and was suspended at a twenty-five degree angle above the floor. Distorted digital images projected onto the screen were intended to add to the sense of disequilibrium, instability and vertigo inherent in the physical component of the installation.

The city, for the first time in its long history, is destructible. A single flight of planes no bigger than a wedge of geese can quickly end this island fantasy, burn the towers, crumble the bridges, turn the underground passages into lethal chambers, cremate the millions. The intimation of mortality is part of New York now: in the sound of jets overhead, in the black headlines of the latest edition.

E.B. White, *Here is New York* (New York: The Curtis Publishing Company, 1949): 50-51.

EcoCité Habitat I
MONTREAL, 2002

ECOCITÉ HABITAT I : 8,000 SF. EIGHT UNIT CONDOMINIUM

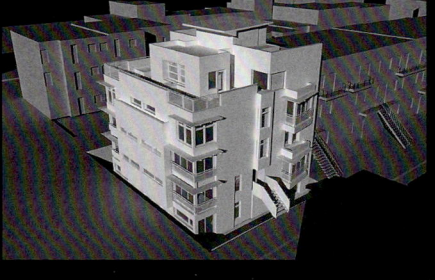

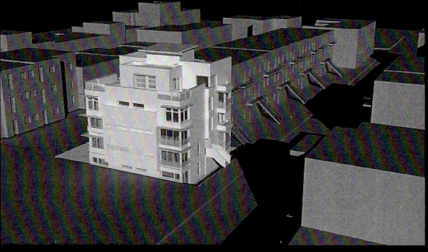

EcoCité Habitat I is an inner-city, environmentally-sensitive condominium project located at the end of a residential block overlooking a neighbourhood park in Point-Saint-Charles, southwest of downtown Montreal. The project is essentially comprised of four 'towers', each of which is divided into two stacked townhouses. All eight units have either a sunken patio at ground level or a planted roof-top terrace. The compact square plan is split by a narrow, sky-lit atrium that acts as a communal space for the residents and as a ventilation plenum. The cubic form is terraced towards the south, with two angled window-boxes on each side and a square projection on its front, the surface of which is designed to receive photovoltaic panels. All the appendages are finished in corrugated metal to match the galvanized exterior metalwork of guards, sun visors and trellises.

Although domestic in scale, the interior finishes specified for the project are decidedly industrial, with polished concrete floors and exposed steel structure. All interior metal work is galvanized and the cabinetry is constructed of exposed straw board. The industrial palette is tempered with reused, sandblasted solid wood doors, re-enameled claw foot metal bathtubs, bamboo flooring and stair treads. In order to reduce toxicity, low VOC paints, sealants, glues and finishes are used. The project also features low-flow faucets and toilets for reduced water consumption. In an effort to dramatically reduce energy consumption, a geo-thermal system was designed for the project, with a radiant heating and cooling system installed in the ceilings of each unit. On the southern exposure, glazing is maximized to insure a high solar gain in winter. In order to control overheating, a *brise-soleil* constructed of folded metal and expanded metal mesh is installed over the windows and heat-mirror films are applied on the west windows. The project is designed to use eighty percent less energy than conventional new construction.

Section A

Section B

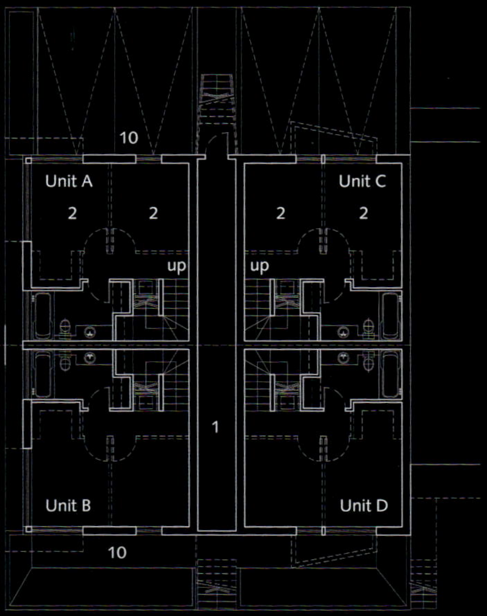

Unit A		Unit C		Unit A	Unit C	Unit E	Unit G
2	2	2	2	4	4	4	2	2

First floor – basement 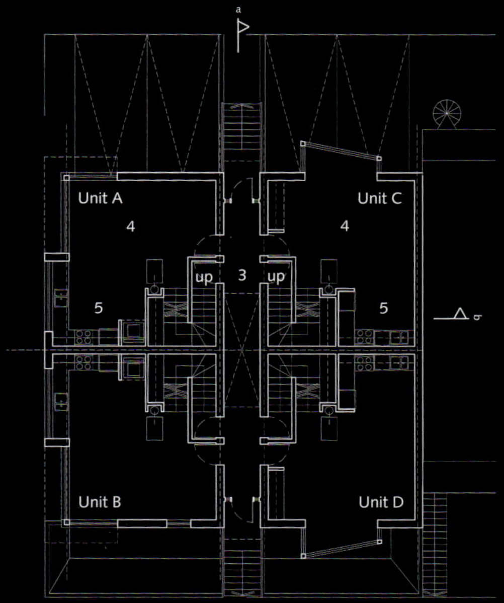 | Second floor 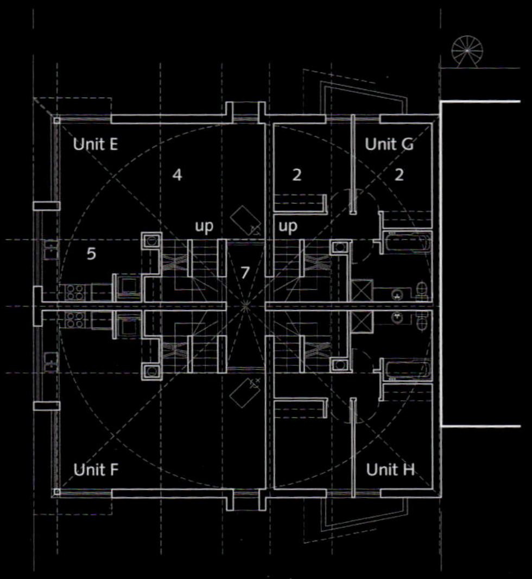 | Third floor

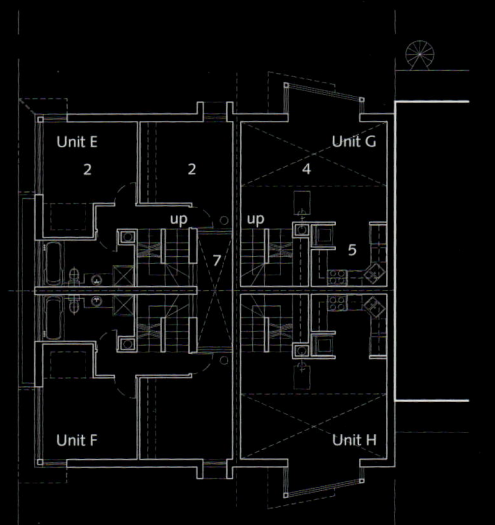

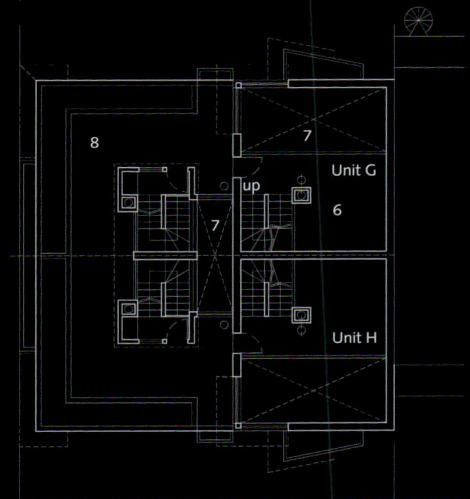

Fourth floor

Fifth floor – mezzanine + roof terrace

1 Mechanical
2 Bedroom
3 Entry atrium
4 Living / dining
5 Kitchen
6 Mezzanine
7 Open
8 Roof terrace
9 Geothermal pipes
10 Patio
11 Low winter sun
12 High summer sun

0   9'   18'

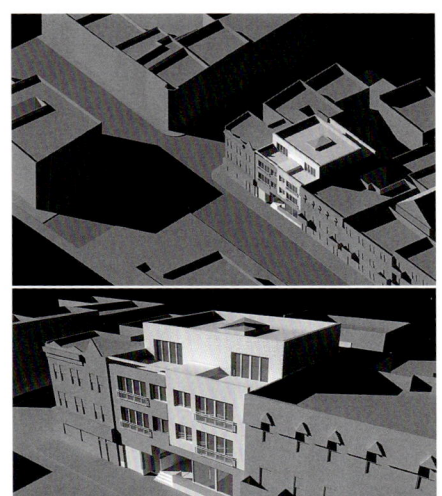

SUPER 8 : *12,000 SF. EIGHT UNIT CONDOMINIUM, RUE AMHERST*

Situated to the east of the Quartier Latin in downtown Montreal, Super 8 is a micro-loft development that consists of eight units that range from five hundred to twelve hundred square feet. The project addresses a need for affordable space in a central location.

The project includes an underground parking garage and storage lockers, plus a two thousand square foot commercial space on the ground floor. The second floor is divided into four studio lofts; the back units enjoy generous balconies, with a stair that leads to a small garden. The upper units have open living, dining and kitchen areas; each has a spiral stair that leads to an enclosed sleeping loft that opens onto a rooftop terrace. The interiors, with their exposed concrete floors (with hot-water radiant heat) and floor-to-ceiling sliding glass doors create a stripped-down architecture that provides an alternative to conventional contractor development in the neighbourhood.

The asymmetrical façade, composed of glazed white and metallic brown brick, separated by the zigzag of a galvanized c-channel, is a 'gestural response' to the dramatic slope of the land directly to the north. Also evident on rue Amherst are the twelve-foot by eight-foot patio doors, with minimized glass guards that allow a full six-foot-wide opening onto the busy street below. The entryway is lined with large-format glazed ceramic tiles that contrast with the corrugated galvalume wall and soffit that extend from the street to the lobby.

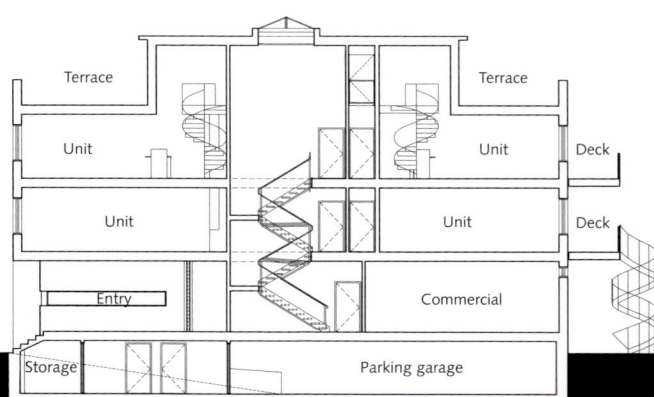

ATELIER BUILD   49

Front elevation – rue Amherst

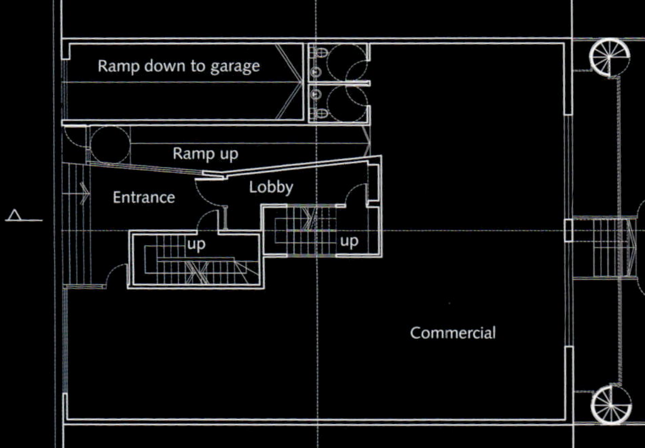

First floor – entry level

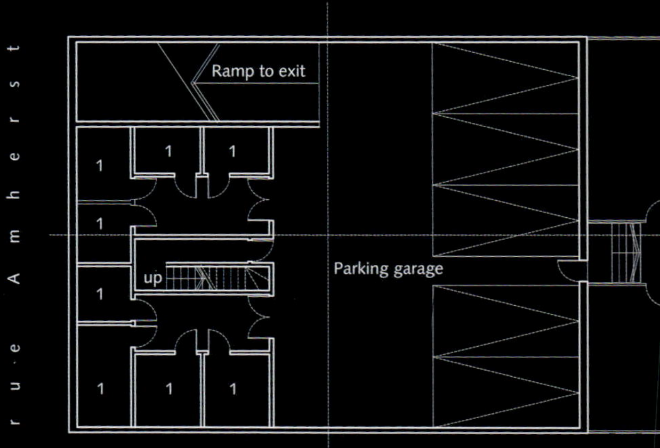

Basement level

rue Amherst

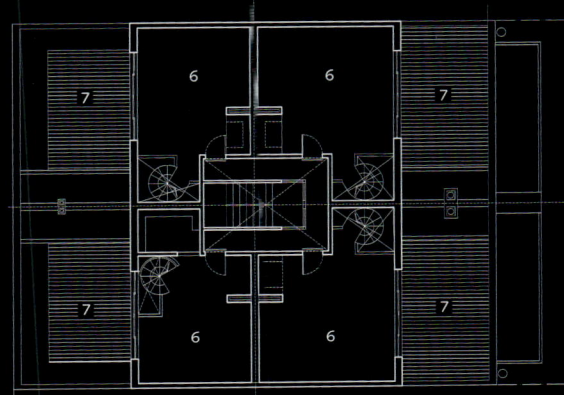
Fourth floor

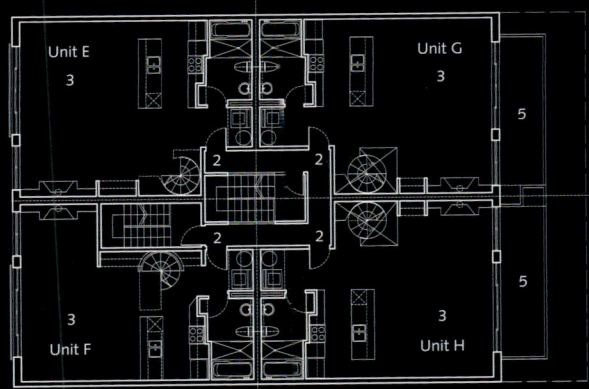
Third floor

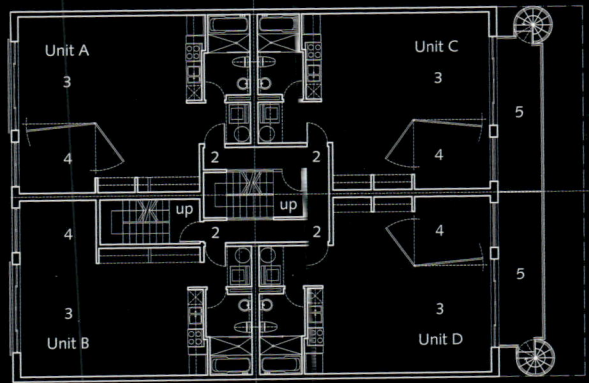
Second floor

@Mentana
MONTREAL, 2008

ATELIER BUILD 53

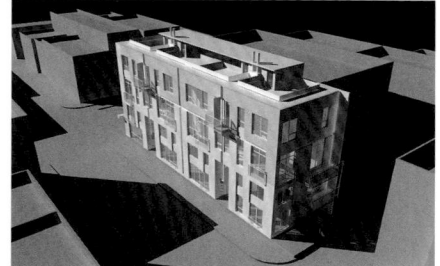

@MENTANA : *10,000 SF. SIX UNIT CONDOMINIUM, RUE DE MENTANA*

Mentana is a six-unit development situated on the southeast corner of rue de Mentana and rue Rachel Est, next to Parc Lafontaine in the Plateau Mont-Royal neighbourhood of Montreal. The project is composed of four towers: the two outer towers each consist of four-storey units; the two middle towers are divided horizontally to form two-storey stacked townhouses. The lower double-height units each feature an integrated volume that includes a sleeping loft; the upper two-storey units are more spacious with an open floor plan for the living, dining and kitchen areas on the main level, with two bedrooms and a double-height bathroom on the upper level. A rooftop terrace with views of Mont Royal to the southwest is accessed from the upper and outer units by four naturally lit stairwells that extend down to the street level entrances.

The envelope of the project is an elongated box that sits on a lot that is twenty-five feet wide and a hundred feet long. It is defined by two double-height portals that provide an entrance to each unit at street level. Each portal is lined with tile that contrasts with the building's two-tone masonry shell. In addition to these incised portals, the project's façade is relieved by a series of galvanized c-channels inscribed into the brick facing, and by four balconies: two project over the sidewalk on rue de Mentana and two extend toward a laneway that forms the southern border of the site.

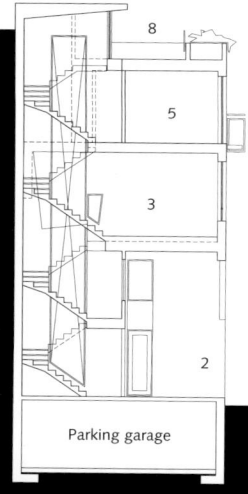

1 Ramp to parking
2 Entry
3 Living / dining
4 Bathroom
5 Bedroom
6 Sleeping mezzanine
7 Open
8 Rooftop terrace
9 Office

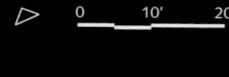

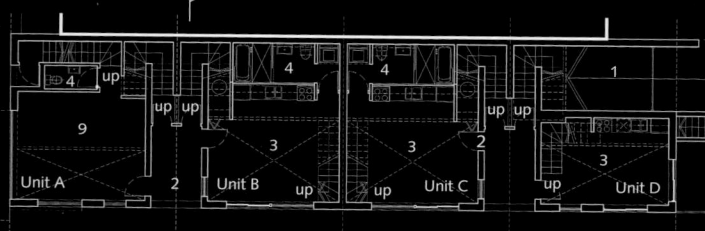

First floor – entry level

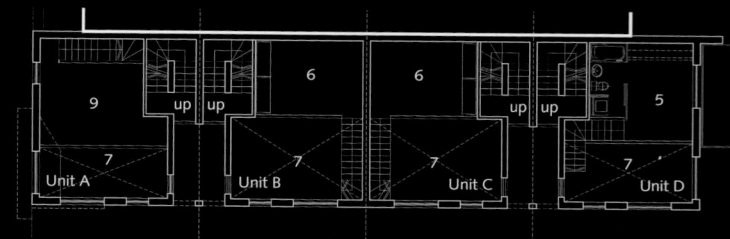

Second floor – mezzanine

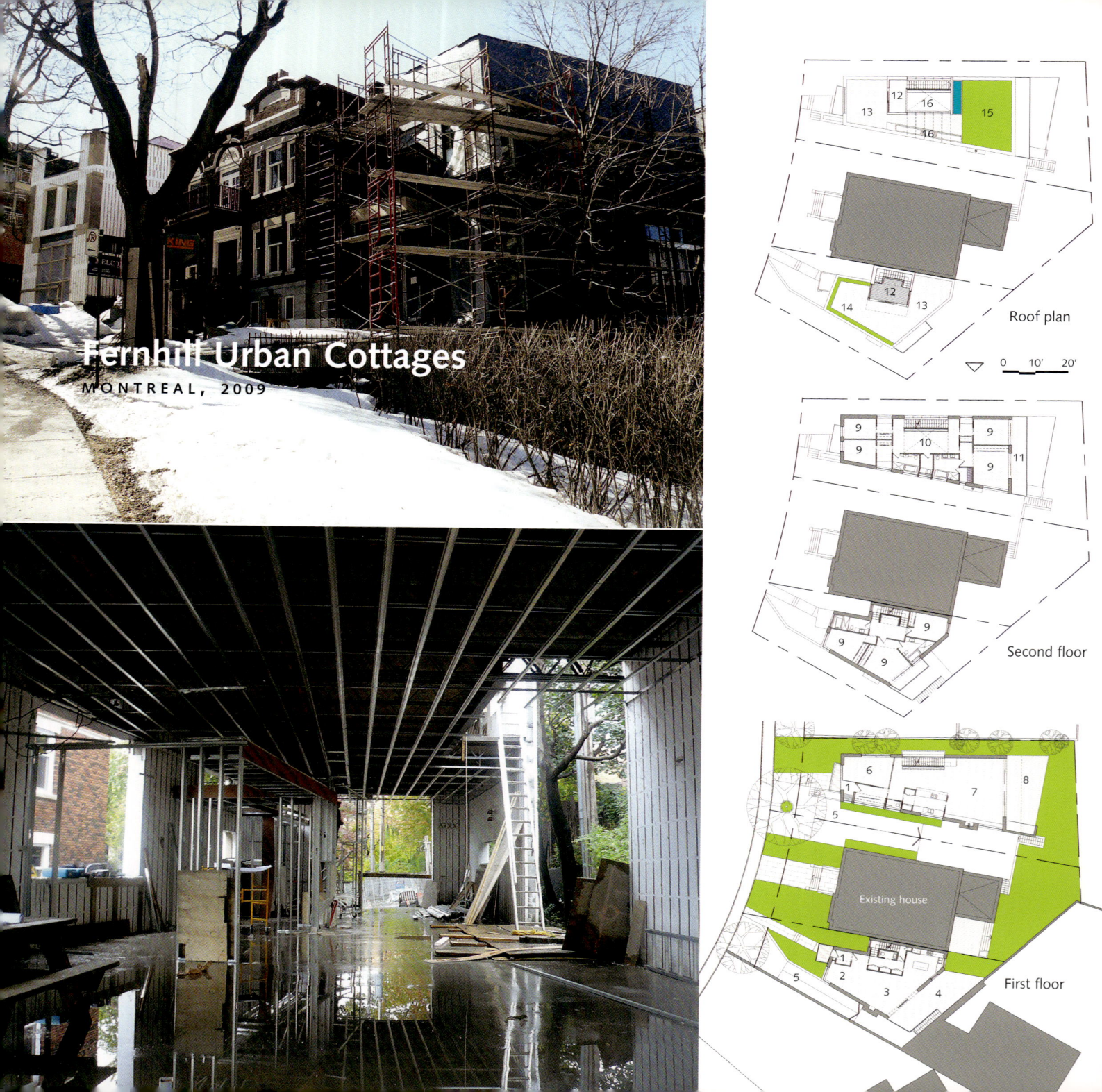

Fernhill Urban Cottages
MONTREAL, 2009

Roof plan

Second floor

First floor

Existing house

FERNHILL COTTAGES : *7,500 SF. TWO UNITS, RUE FERNHILL*

The project consists of two cottages, one detached and one attached, which are located on either side of an extensively renovated 1920's house. Situated just below Mont-Royal Park, the site slopes steeply and is defined by retaining walls along the southern and northern borders of the lot. The project maximizes the allowable buildable area of the site which consists of three divided lots. The result is two trapezoidal volumes (one more elongated than the other) with large expanses of floor-to-ceiling glazing and elongated ribbon windows incised within each project's masonry exterior.

Visually and architecturally, the project forms a decidedly contemporary contrast to the surrounding structures. On the south wall of the upper cottage, a curtain wall system and skylight maximize solar gain and are aligned with the house's triple-height atrium. The atrium is passively ventilated and features a planted trellis on its exterior with a vertical vegetal screen on the interior that lines one side of a folded metal stair. Each cottage also features a planted roof with expanses of cedar decking and reflecting pools. Full access to the roof allows immediate views of the mountain and, to the east, the urban landscape of Plateau Mont-Royal.

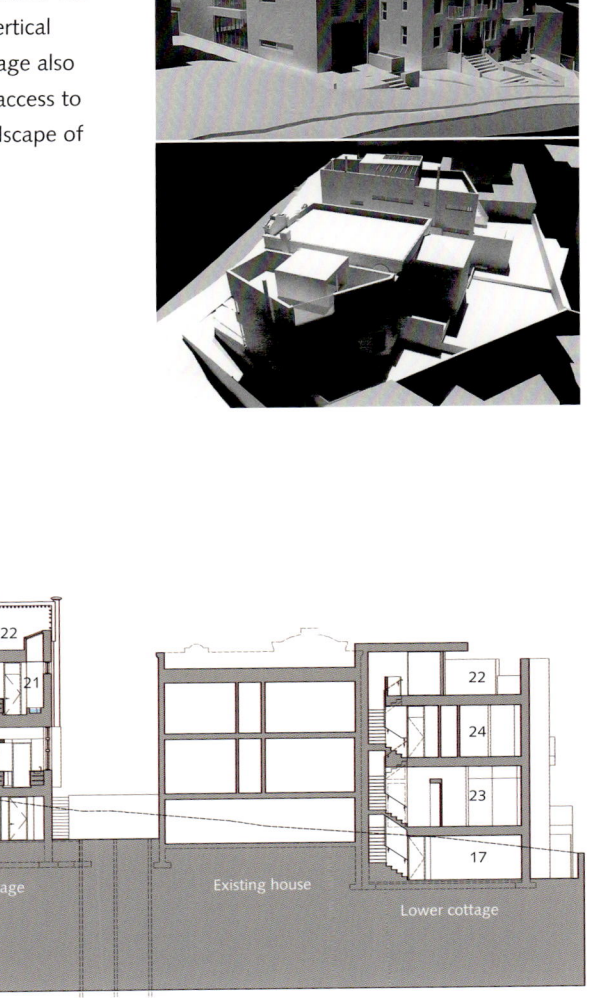

1   Entry
2   Dining
3   Living
4   Patio (carport below)
5   Ramp (down to parking)
6   Studio / office
7   Living / dining (garage below)
8   Patio
9   Bedroom
10 Sunroom
11 Balcony
12 Sunroom
13 Roof terrace
14 Planted perimeter
15 Planted roof
16 Skylights

17 Media room
18 Bio wall
19 Sunroom
20 Operable window
21 Bath with skylight
22 Roof terrace
23 Living room
24 Bedroom

Postscript

Michael Carroll and Danita Rooyakkers were both students at the Technical University of Nova Scotia in the late 1980s. Michael, from Notre Dame Bay, Newfoundland, and Danita, who grew up in Cape Breton after moving from Holland, showed a natural inclination toward an urbanist approach to architecture. Their interest in the making of the 'good city' has subsequently become a principal focus of the work of Atelier Build.

After working with me in Halifax, Michael moved to Montreal where he formed Atelier Build with Danita in 1995. They began practicing and have created a series of convincing infill housing projects in the city.

Each of the projects references an urban type, yet each is also a unique architectural piece that enriches a distinctive urban fabric.

The work of Atelier Build highlights a new, developing and optimistic model for architectural practice that promises to underline the fit between the world of ideas and the world of things.

Brian MacKay-Lyons

Acknowledgements

Atelier Build would like to thank Dalhousie University's Faculty of Architecture and Planning, and Brian Carter for including us in this new series that focuses on emerging Canadian practices. We studied at the Technical University of Nova Scotia in the 1980s, when Dr. Essy Baniassad was Dean, and Brian MacKay-Lyons was a young practitioner and professor, fresh from UCLA. Both of us would like to acknowledge their influence on how we think about and build architecture.

Many people have been instrumental in Atelier Build's success. Attila Tolnai plays a critical role as project director/manager in the realization of our projects. His engineering background and influence of analytic philosophy have brought invaluable insight to the design process. Attila was largely responsible for the property development and construction processes of the projects.

For the later and larger projects that include Eco-Cité Habitat I, Super 8, @Mentana and the Fernhill Urban Cottages, Jean-François Lavigne, as project architect, has proven his technical and practical prowess in the production of the construction documents. Appreciative thanks are also due to the many consultants and trades that have given their expertise, and to the people and institutions who have been involved in the financing of the projects.

We would like to thank the Canadian Centre for Architecture for their recognition of our work and their support of us as part of the emerging Montreal design scene – our inclusion in the post-9-11 exhibition, *Laboratoire*, was a defining moment.

As Prix de Rome recipients in 2004, we would like to thank the Canada Council for the Arts for their support, with special thanks to Brigitte Desrochers. The award allowed Atelier Build to research buildings in the high-density, urban areas of Italy, Japan and the Netherlands. The publication of this book was also made possible through a grant from the Canada Council, for which we are grateful.

In addition, Michael would like to acknowledge McGill University, Syracuse University and Southern Polytechnic State University in Atlanta for providing the opportunity to explore architecture through teaching and research and to help bridge the divide between 'thinking and making'.

The world of architecture has brought us friends who have supported our work in many ways over the years. In particular, we would like to acknowledge Dan Anderson for naming us Build, and Helen Bowers, Marta Franco, Terrance Galvin, Wayne Guy, Andrew King, Brenda Webster-Tweel and Peter Yeadon, for their intelligence and support along the way.

A special thanks to the graduate architects we have employed periodically over the years, to Carla Norman for helping with the text and to Donald Westin at Tuns Press for his work on this book.

Michael Carroll
Danita Rooyakkers

Exhibitions

Home Turf
"Fernhill Urban Cottages"
Syracuse University School of Architecture,
Syracuse, New York
Faculty Show, March-April 2009.

Canada Goes Wild! (Sponsored by Design Exchange, Toronto)
Canadian Embassy, Tokyo, Japan +
Canadian Pavilion, AICHI World EXPO 2005, Nagoya, Japan
Group Exhibition + Catalogue, April 2005.

CCA Laboratoire (Curators: Mark Wigley + Frédéric Migayrou)
"code : zero"
Canadian Centre of Architecture,
Montreal, Quebec
Group Exhibition, April 2002.

ARTCITY: Emerging Canadian Architecture
The Calgary Institute for Modern Art,
Calgary, Alberta
Group Exhibition, September 2001.

Canadian Architecture: 16 Architectures
Sponsored by CANUK
Manifesto 1998,
Edinburgh, Scotland, September 1998;
Royal Institute of British Architects,
London, England, June 1998;
Canada House, London, May 1998.

Published Projects

"Building Design", Property Development + Progressive Architecture, *Architectural Design*, London, 2004.

"Building/Art", University of Calgary Press, November 2003.

"Laboratories: Code Zero", AI, (Architecture and Ideas), Vol.1V, No.1, 2003.

"The End of Imagination?" *ARCHIS*, 2002.

"Musing on the Sept. 11 Challenge", *Globe and Mail*, February 2002.

"The New City House", Taunton Press, Spring 2002.

"Montreal: Living in a Boîte", *Dwell* magazine, February 2002.

"Outside the Box", *Canadian Architect*, October 2001.

"Slender Side Split", *Canadian Architect*, July 1998.

Credits

Thin House, av de L'Hotel-de-Ville, Montreal
Construction completion: 1996
Designers: Atelier Build
Developer: Build Inc.
Structural Engineer: Mario Gendron
Contractor: Bosses Construction

Tower House, av Laval, Montreal
Construction completion: 1997
Designers: Atelier Build
Structural Engineer: Gino Lanni
Developer/Contractor: Build Inc.

Back House, rue Saint-Christophe, Montreal
Construction completion: 1998
Designers: Atelier Build
Structural Engineer: Gino Lanni
Developer/Contractor: Build Inc.

Box House, rue Saint-Christophe, Montreal
Construction completion: 2000
Designers: Atelier Build
Structural Engineer: Gino Lanni
Developer/Contractor: Build Inc.

Code Zero, Canadian Centre for Architecture
Installation completion: 2002
Designers: Atelier Build and Wayne Guy
Installation: Michael Carroll + Geoff Crosby
Digital projection (as shown in photographs): Adad Hannah

EcoCité Habitat I, rue Coleraine, Montreal
Construction completion: 2002
Designers: Atelier Build
Architect: Zaraté + Lavigne Architects
Developer: Christopher Holmes, EcoCité Developments
Environmental Consultant: Greg Allen, Sustainable Edge, Toronto
Structural Engineer: Gino Lanni
Contractor: Build Inc.

Super 8, rue Amherst, Montreal
Construction completion: 2004
Designers: Atelier Build
Architect: Zaraté + Lavigne Architects
Structural Engineer: Gino Lanni
Developer/Contractor: Build Inc.

Mentana, rue Rachel est, Montreal
Construction completion: 2008
Designers: Atelier Build
Architect: Zaraté + Lavigne Architects
Developer: Build Inc.
Structural Engineer: Avnish Rughani
Contractor: Melcon

Fernhill, av Fernhill, Montreal
Projected completion: 2009
Designers: Atelier Build
Architect: Zaraté + Lavigne Architects
Developer: Build Inc.
Structural Engineer: Avnish Rughani
Contractor: Melcon

Image credits

All drawings & renderings by Atelier Build.

Aux Quatre Points Cardinaux Inc.
4-5 aerial photo.

Michael Carroll
11, 12, 15, 19 top, 20 top left, 22, 24, 25, 28, 29, 40, 49 inset, 50 top, 51 bottom, 53 inset, 56.

Brigitte Desrochers
30, 32, 34, 35.

Alain Laforest
cover, 16, 17, 23, 26, 27, 31, 38, 39, 41, 42-43, 44, 45, 46, 47, 48, 49 background, 50 bottom, 51 top.

Michel Legendre
36, 37.

David Duncan Livingston
8, 19 bottom, 20 except top left, 21.

Mathieu Manikowski
52, 53 except inset, 55.

Notes

Michael Carroll and Danita Rooyakkers are the principals of Atelier Build.

Danita Rooyakkers and Attila Tolnai are the principals of Build Inc.

Jean-François Lavigne is project architect with Zaraté + Lavigne Architects.

Contributors

Brian Carter is an architect who worked in practice with Arup in London prior to taking up an academic appointment in the USA. He is currently Dean of the School of Architecture & Urban Planning at SUNY Buffalo. His work has been published in numerous international journals, including *Casabella*, *Detail*, *AD* and *The Architectural Review*. The author of several books, Brian Carter also initiated the MAP series, which received an AIA International Book Award.

Brian MacKay-Lyons received his BArch from TUNS in 1978 and his MArchUD at UCLA. He founded Brian MacKay-Lyons Architecture Urban Design in 1985, and twenty years later, partnered with Talbot Sweetapple to form MacKay-Lyons Sweetapple Architects. He is a leading proponent of regionalist architecture and this recognition has prompted an increase in public and international commissions. Brian is the Director of the Ghost Architectural Laboratory and a Professor of Architecture at Dalhousie University.

Grant Wanzel is a Professor in the Faculty of Architecture and Planning at Dalhousie University, where he served as Dean from 2003 to 2008. A co-partner with the Design Co-op and the Community Habitat & Resource Team, he has served on the boards of numerous organizations including the National Housing Committee of the Canadian Council on Social Development and the Canadian Housing and Renewal Association. He was awarded the CMHC's National Social Housing Award in 1999 and the CMHC Volunteer of the Year award for 2001.